HIP-HOP & R&B

Culture, Music & Storytelling

John Legend

HIP-HOP & R&B

Culture, Music & Storytelling

Beyonce

Bruno Mars

Cardi B

Chance the Rapper

DJ Khaled

Drake

Jay-Z

John Legend

Lil Wayne

Nicki Minaj

Pharrell

Pitbull

Post Malone

Rihanna

The Weeknd

Travis Scott

MASON CREST

Carlie Lawson

HIP-HOP & R&B

John Legend

Culture, Music & Storytelling

MASON CREST

450 Parkway Drive, Suite D, Broomall, Pennsylvania 19008
(866) MCP-BOOK (toll-free) • www.masoncrest.com

Printed in the United States of America

First printing
9 8 7 6 5 4 3 2 1

ISBN (hardback) 978-1-4222-4364-0
ISBN (ebook) 978-1-4222-7443-9

Cataloging-in-Publication Data on file with the Library of Congress

**NATIONAL
HIGHLIGHTS**

Developed and produced by National Highlights Inc.
Editor: Dave Johnstone
Production: Michelle Luke
Interior and cover design: Annalisa Gumbrecht, Studio Gumbrecht

QR CODES AND LINKS TO THIRD-PARTY CONTENT

CONTENTS

KEY ICONS TO LOOK OUT FOR:

Words to Understand: These words with their easy-to-understand definitions will increase the reader's understanding of the text while building vocabulary skills.

Sidebars: This boxed material within the main text allows readers to build knowledge, gain insights, explore possibilities, and broaden their perspectives by weaving together additional information to provide realistic and holistic perspectives.

Educational Videos: Readers can view videos by scanning our QR codes, providing them with additional educational content to supplement the text. Examples include news coverage, moments in history, speeches, iconic sports moments, and much more!

Text-Dependent Questions: These questions send the reader back to the text for more careful attention to the evidence presented there.

Research Projects: Readers are pointed toward areas of further inquiry connected to each chapter. Suggestions are provided for projects that encourage deeper research and analysis.

Series Glossary of Key Terms: This back-of-the-book glossary contains terminology used throughout this series. Words found here increase the reader's ability to read and comprehend higher-level books and articles in this field.

John Legend

HIP-HOP & R&B

Chapter 1

Career Highlights—
Setting Recording Industry Records

With his win of an Emmy in 2018 for his portrayal of Christ in the televised live theater production of *Jesus Christ Superstar*, John Legend became the first man of African American heritage to achieve EGOT status. That name stands for having won an Emmy, Grammy, Oscar, and Tony award. His music has won him 10 Grammy awards. His song "Glory," for the soundtrack of the film *Selma*, won him his Oscar. He won a Tony award for his work as co-producer of the Broadway production *Jitney*.

Legend has released twelve albums to date. They are a mixture of self-released CDs and record label releases, including three extended plays, four live albums, six studio albums, and two video albums. He has released thirty-eight singles.

Before he ever released an album, Legend became known as songwriter through his

John Legend at the 2018 Creative Arts Emmy Awards where he won an Emmy for *Jesus Christ Superstar*.

Scan here to watch "Stereo." John Legend met his future wife, model Chrissy Teigen, while making it. The video features Teigen as his love interest.

collaborations with established artists like Kanye West and guest appearances singing with performers like Alicia Keys. Before his debut CD, he'd recorded with Lauryn Hill and Jay-Z among others. His single "All of Me" topped the Billboard Hot 100 chart. It has been Legend's sole number-one hit to date.

All Released Solo Albums to Date:
Discography

JOHN STEPHENS
(Released 2000)

John Legend's first release was a self-produced and self-published one under his birth name. It allowed him to shop his songwriting and offered an opportunity to educate record executives about his developing talents as a gospel-infused rhythm and blues artist. Few copies of the original release remain, but the tracks were later re-released under his pseudonym before he was signed to a record deal.

LIVE AT JIMMY'S UPTOWN
(Released 2001)

Like many artists today, John Legend began his career by self-producing and self-publishing his early works. Legend recorded many of his early shows and released them as live CDs. This CD contains material recorded at Jimmy's Uptown in 2001.

John Legend—Live at SOB's
(Released June 10, 2003)

John Legend's initial release offered the ten tracks of music recorded before a live, studio audience. He self-released the CD on his own label.

At the time, the artist performed under his given name, John Stephens. The first pressing of "Live at SOB's" featured what is now referred to as a bonus track, "Without You." All songs on the CD were recorded at the club SOB's in New York City during two performances—on June 28, 2002, and December 6, 2002.

Beginning with its second pressing, the CD carried the musician's pseudonym, John Legend, and dropped the tenth track, "Without You." Most of the songs Legend wrote himself working with Dave Tozer and Kayne West, however, the CD does include one traditional folk song and one cover song. The artist performed his and Tozer's arrangement of the traditional song "Motherless Chile." The CD also includes Legend's cover of the 1983 Talking Heads' hit "Burning Down the House." The original pressing of the CD has become a collector's item and sells for a higher price than standard copies of the CD.

Get Lifted
(Released December 28, 2004)

Produced by Kanye West, this album was Legend's first studio release. It came out on West's

Scan here to watch "Glory," Legend's highly acclaimed single for the film *Selma*, performed live at the Oscars ceremony.

GOOD Muscle label, a subsidiary of Sony Urban Music on Columbia Records. It sold 3 million copies worldwide, 2.1 million of which were U.S. sales, which earned it double platinum status. Legend came out of the gate strong, winning the 2006 Grammy for Best R&B Album for *Get Lifted*. It also netted him the Best New Artist Grammy that year and the Grammy for Best Male R&B Vocal Performance for the album single "Ordinary People."

Collaborations

- "Number One," featuring Kanye West.
- "So High," featuring Lauryn Hill.
- "I Can Change," featuring Snoop Dogg.
- "It Don't Have to Change," featuring the Stephens Family.
- "Live It Up," featuring Miri Ben-Ari.

JOHN LEGEND—SOLO SESSIONS VOL. 1: LIVE AT THE KNITTING FACTORY
(Released August 29, 2005)

Legend also self-released his second CD, *John Legend—Solo Sessions Vol. 1: Live at The Knitting Factory*. It featured a couple of cover songs and much of the artist's own writing. Legend attributes his song writing using his given last name of Stephens while he releases albums using his pseudonym. His second release continued his

John Legend at the twentieth Annual Soul Train Music Awards in 2006 where he won an award.

John Legend and Usher at the 2012 Billboard Music Awards.

Scan here to watch the official music video for John Legend's "Green Light," featuring André 3000.

songwriting collaborations with Kayne West and Dave Tozer. The covers include the Marvin Gaye song, "If This World Were Mine" and the Lauren Hill and Kanye West song "All Falls Down." This CD also includes the traditional song "Motherless Chile," which was originally on his *Live at SOB's* release.

ONCE AGAIN
(Released October 24, 2006)

Legend's second studio release on Columbia Records provided him more creative freedom. He co-wrote most of its music and co-produced the album. Rather than featuring other performers on the album's singles, Legend sampled artists including the Four Tops and the Icemen featuring Jimi Hendrix. His songwriting partners for the CD included Kanye West, Dave Tozer, and Estelle Swaray. Will.i.am produced multiple tracks on the CD, and while Kanye West retained the executive production credit, Legend moved into the second position with his sophomore effort. *Once Again* has sold more than 2.5 million copies worldwide, with more than one million copies sold in the U.S., earning it platinum status.

Collaborations

- "Save Room," featuring samples from "Stormy," performed by Gábor Szabó.
- "Heaven," featuring samples from "Heaven Only Knows," performed by Monk Higgins.

John Legend HIP-HOP & R&B

- "Each Day Gets Better," featuring samples from "In These Changing Times," performed by The Four Tops.
- "Slow Dance," featuring samples from "She's a Fox," performed by the Icemen featuring Jimi Hendrix.
- "Another Again," featuring samples from "Lost for Words," performed by Midnight Movers Unlimited.

LIVE AT THE TIN ANGEL: LEGEND NETWORK CD VOLUME 1
(Released 2007)

John Legend enjoys giving back to his fans with music. In the case of *Live at the Tin Angel: Legend Network CD Volume 1,* he recorded his set at

Scan here to watch the official music video for John Legend's "Tonight (Best You Ever Had)" featuring Ludacris.

John Legend performs at the Orlando Stadium for the FIFA World Cup Kick-off Celebration Concert in 2010, in Johannesburg, South Africa.

Scan here to watch the official music video for John Legend's "Save Room."

Brandy collaborated with Legend on his Album *Evolver*.

the Tin Angel on November 21, 2001, and chose five tracks to issue this EP. It features live versions of "Something For Nothing," "Must Be The Way," "Stay With You," "Soul Joint," and "Sun Comes Up." It also features a bonus track, a rough cut of "Again." Like many of Legend's releases, this one was self-released. He issued it as a gift to members of the Legend Network, his fan club, in its first year of existence, 2007.

EVOLVER
(Released October 28, 2008)

Legend experimented with his sound on *Evolver*, his third studio album. He admitted to the press that the CD departed from his original sound.

In it, he used ample synthesizers and numerous guest performers. This CD features performances by André 3000, Brandy, Estelle, and Kanye West. Legend largely departed from breakup songs and romantic ballads on this release and filled it with tropical, reggae-influenced tracks and soulful soft rock.

Collaborations

- "Green Light," featuring André 3000.
- "No Other Love," featuring Estelle.
- "It's Over," featuring Kanye West.
- "Quickly," featuring Brandy.

LIVE FROM PHILADELPHIA
(Released January 15, 2008)

Legend released the CD *Live from Philadelphia* as an exclusive in Target stores only. Target was also the only store to offer the CD/DVD version, although other outlets offered the DVD-only version. Legend performs a diverse set, representing his best-known tracks from his studio albums. He throws in two cover songs—"Dance to the Music" by Sly and the Family Stone and the Beatles' "I Want You (She's So Heavy)." He also integrates the Blackbyrds' release "Rock Creek Park"

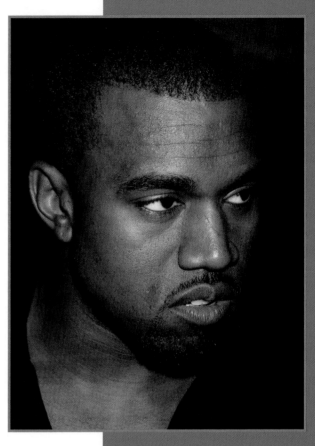

Kanye West and John Legend have worked together often. West features on *Evolver*.

into his single "P.D.A. (We Just Don't Care)." The album displays why Legend is known for showstopping performances.

LEGEND NETWORK: JOHN LEGEND 2008
(Released 2008)

The limited special-edition release *Legend Network: John Legend 2008* was never sold in stores or online. Legend self-released it as a gift to his fans who had joined his fan club, the "Legend Network." In a note enclosed with the CD, he thanked Network fans, referring to them as "a positive group of people supporting my music." Various special events were held for Legend

John Legend performs for *Good Morning America* in Central Park in 2013.

John Legend and his wife Chrissy Teigen arrive at the
White House Correspondents Dinner in 2012.

Network fans, including the "King & Queen" fellowship event and concert in Philadelphia on July 26, 2007, which the artist recorded. He then created this CD recording from that performance.

WAKE UP!
(Released September 21, 2010)

Wake Up! represents Legend's love for covers, his growing political awareness, and his natural tendency to collaborate. He partners with the band The Roots on the soul-infused CD inspired by the 2008 Barack Obama presidential campaign and developing social climate. The album features artists Black Thought, C.L. Smooth, Common, Malik Yusef, and Melanie Fiona, updating and reinterpreting songs from the 1960s and 1970s. It includes "Wake Up Everybody," the January 1976 number one R&B single by Harold Melvin & the Blue Notes and "Compared to What" by Eugene McDaniels. Other gritty tracks by Curtis Mayfield and Marvin Gaye round out the eleven covers on the release. Legend contributes one original composition, "Shine." The album succeeds as an attempt to

John Legend was inspired by Barack Obama's presidential campaign. It led to him making the album *Wake Up!*

John Legend   HIP-HOP & R&B

introduce the music of tumultuous, changing times to the generations benefitting from the implementation of those changes. Despite being essentially a cover album, its thought provoking, cohesive grittiness earned it the 2010 Grammy for Best R&B Album.

Collaborations

- "Hard Times," featuring Black Thought.
- "Wake Up Everybody," featuring Common and Melanie Fiona.
- "Our Generation (The Hope of the World)," featuring CL Smooth.
- "Little Ghetto Boy (Prelude)," featuring Malik Yusef.

LOVE IN THE FUTURE
(Released September 2, 2013)

Three years following the massive collaborative project, Legend released a decidedly solo album, *Love in the Future*. Like earlier releases, Kanye West steps in as executive producer and Legend co-writes with numerous people. The CD features a lush, sophisticated sound instrumented

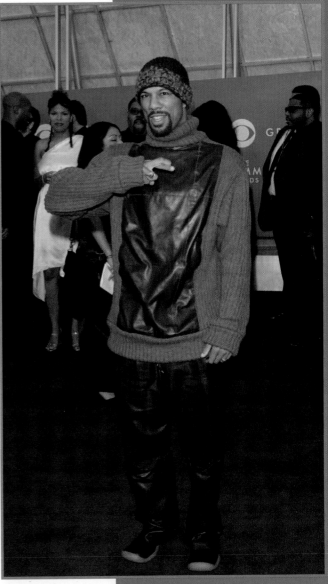

Rapper Common collaborated with John Legend on the album *Wake Up!*

through piano, percussion, and strings. More so than previous releases, each track seems crafted for the artist's voice, even his cover of Bobby Caldwell's single, "Open Your Eyes." As hinted in the title, the subject matter of the CD revolves around love. Filled with ballads, Legend crafts a release meant to cross genres and cultures with its sixteen songs. A deluxe edition of the CD provides four extra tracks.

Common and John Legend at the eighty-seventh annual Academy Awards. They won an Oscar for "Glory" from the movie *Selma*.

John Legend

HIP-HOP & R&B

Collaborations

- "Who Do We Think We Are," featuring Rick Ross.
- "Angel (Interlude)," featuring Stacy Barthe.

DARKNESS AND LIGHT
(Released December 2, 2016)

With *Darkness and Light,* Legend switches to using a single producer for the majority of the tracks—Blake Mills. This results in an album co-written by Mills with him playing various instruments on the CD. Together, the pair merge adult pop, gospel, folk, and rhythm & blues to create the antithesis of *Love in the Future.* Diverging from his conventional ballads, the CD offers singles like "Penthouse Floor," featuring Chance the Rapper. The funky track examines the African American struggle for equality from a working-class perspective, the goal being success of the level that gets each person to the penthouse floor. While he does deposit a few ballads, the CD focuses its music more on issues. This also includes "Overload," a track analyzing the effect of fans and the press on an individual and how their insatiable curiosity

Chance the Rapper collaborated with John Legend on "Penthouse Floor" from the *Darkness and Light* album.

damages the object of their curiosity. Legend also addresses life as a parent on this release, dedicating its most touching ballad not to his wife or a former lover, but to his young daughter.

Collaborations

- "Penthouse Floor," featuring Chance the Rapper.
- "Darkness and Light," featuring Brittany Howard.
- "Overload," featuring Miguel.

Blues singer Brittany Howard sang on "Darkness and Light."

A Legendary Christmas Album
(Released October 26, 2018)

John Legend focuses on his faith and family with his Christmas album. While it is common for major artists to release at least one Christmas CD, in Legend's case, it dovetails with his career prior to that of recording artist—as choir and musical director for a church. He served as a music minister for about nine years. His celebration of the holiday includes both secular and religious tracks. Fans may want to opt for the physical CD rather than the digital release, since it comes with a booklet filled with the artist's family photos. The tracks mix covers from the 1940s to the 1970s with original compositions like "Wrap Me Up in Your Love." The tracks offer a Motown-flavored mix with "Purple Snowflakes," also known as "Pretty Little Baby."

A television special also accompanied the CD release. Legend tapped the talents of wife Chrissy Teigen to co-host the NBC production, *A Legendary Christmas with John and Chrissy*. Teigen also had opportunity to contribute vocals in their caroling scenes with guests Darren Criss, Jane Lynch, Raphael Saadiq, and Meghan Trainor. The massive TV special also included appearances by Awkwafina, Ben Schwartz, Derek Hough, Kenan Thompson, Kim Kardashian West, Neal Brennan, Kris Jenner, Retta, Sam Richardson, Yassir Lester, Zach Galifianakis, and The Fab Five From "Queer Eye" —Antoni Porowski, Tan France, Karamo Brown, Bobby Berk, and Jonathan Van Ness.

Collaborations

- "What Christmas Means to Me," featuring Stevie Wonder.
- "Have Yourself a Merry Little Christmas," featuring Esperanza Spalding.

VIDEO ALBUMS

Long before he had a television special, Legend released two video albums. The first of these he released on November 22, 2005, *John*

Scan the code to watch John Legend's "Penthouse Floor," featuring Chance the Rapper.

Legend: Live at the House of Blues. He followed it three years later with the April 8, 2008, release of *John Legend: Live from Philadelphia*. Much of the artist's work is influenced by the state of Pennsylvania. That's because he attended college in that state and served as the music and choir director at Bethel A.M.E. Church in Scranton, Pennsylvania, for nine years. Although he grew up in Ohio, it was in Pennsylvania that he built his early fan following, and he often revisits the area to record live shows before his adopted hometown crowd.

John Legend attended the University of Pennsylvania in Philadelphia.

The Inside Skinny on Some Major Collaborations

With each album and special appearance John Legend illustrates his love of all music. The diversity of his collaborations shows his willingness to explore new sounds and work with new people. While he often collaborates with friend Kanye West, he also searches out other musicians and songwriters in a variety of genres.

John Legend HIP-HOP & R&B

Darkness and Light by John Legend, produced by Blake Mills
(Released December 2, 2016)

Mills told *Billboard* magazine that he and Legend had met and agreed that "There were not going to be any songs about nothing on the record. And there was not going to be a single moment for which there wasn't an artistic reason."

Jesus Christ Superstar with Sara Bareilles
(Broadcast 2018)

"He's just phenomenal… It's so rare that anyone is given such a unique instrument. His voice is . . . there's no one who sounds like John Legend. [It's] his command over his voice, and he's throwing himself into this [role] so wholeheartedly," Bareilles, who played the role of Mary Magdalene, told *E! Online*.

Duets with Bridget Carrington
(Broadcast 2018)

"His voice—it's so smooth and his technique—I'm just trying to get like him," Carrington told ABC News.

Sara Bareilles and John Legend attend the 2018 Tribeca Film Festival. They worked together on *Jesus Christ Superstar*.

Scan the code to watch John Legend's "BloodPop—A Good Night" featuring BloodPop.

Tours Completed

John Legend has completed five major tours of his own as headliner. He also has toured as a supporting act for other artists, including Alicia Keys on her *Diary* Tour.

THE *GET LIFTED* TOUR

In 2005, the singer/songwriter embarked on his first headlining tour in support of his debut album *Get Lifted*. It was a North American tour.

THE *ONCE AGAIN* TOUR

Legend again hit the road in 2007, in support of his sophomore studio effort, *Once Again*. This also was a North American tour. The performance from *Live from Philadelphia* comes from this tour.

THE *EVOLVER*

The artist's 2009 tour in support of his third studio release, *Evolver*, also included only North America dates.

THE *LOVE IN THE FUTURE* WORLD TOUR

After a five-year break from the road, Legend returned to live performances in 2014. He hit the road for the *Love in the Future* tour. It was his first world tour as a headliner.

THE *DARKNESS AND LIGHT* WORLD TOUR

After another three-year break, John Legend conducted another world tour in support of his *Darkness and Light* tour. In 2017, the artist embarked on his second headlining world tour.

John Legend performing at Rock in Rio in 2015, in the city of Rio de Janeiro, Brazil.

A cappella: A vocal musical performance with no instrumental accompaniment.

Corps: An organized group of people engaged in a specific activity. A corps may be civil or military in nature.

Session musician: A musician hired to perform during a recording session or live performance who can sight-read music. They are usually familiar with multiple genres of music. Also called a "backing musician" or "studio musician."

Chrissie Teigen and John Legend at the GQ Men of the Year Awards in 2018, at the Tate Modern, London.

Chapter 2

The Road to the Top—
Fulfilling a Lifelong Dream

Family Life

John Legend, born John Roger Stephens, in Springfield, Ohio, to working-class parents, beat the odds to graduate from high school and then from an Ivy League university. Now a successful actor, singer, and songwriter, he came into this world on December 28, 1978, born to Phyllis Elaine (Lloyd), a seamstress, and Ronald Lamar Stephens, a factory worker at International Harvester. He has one sibling, a brother, Vaughn Anthony Stephens, who performs as Vaughn Anthony.

At first, his mother homeschooled him to allow him to advance his studies and devote time to musical study. He began singing with the church choir at age four. His grandmother began teaching him piano when he reached the age of

John Legend and his mother at the House of Hype Grammy Weekend, in 2007, at the Roosevelt Hotel, Hollywood, CA.

seven. He did move into the public school system eventually, attending Springfield North High School from the ages of 12 to 16. He graduated as the class salutatorian in 1994. He matriculated to the University of Pennsylvania and earned a degree in English with an emphasis on African American literature in 1999.

Legend served as the musical director and president of Counterparts, a coed jazz and pop **a cappella** group. Counterparts cut records, including a cover of Joan Osborne's "One of Us," with Legend on lead vocals. The track appeared on the 1998 *Best of Collegiate a Cappella* compilation CD.

In 2007, on the set of the video for his single "Studio," he met model Chrissy Teigen. Legend proposed, and Teigen accepted, while the couple vacationed in the Maldives in 2011. They married on September 14, 2013, in Como, Italy. The couple have two children, a daughter, Luna Simone, born April 14, 2016, and a son, Miles Theodore, born May 16, 2018.

John and Chrissy were married in 2013 in Italy. They have two children.

Discovery

Legend met Lauryn Hill when he accompanied a friend to an audition. The friend raved about Legend's piano prowess, prompting Hill to ask him to play for her. His impromptu performance netted him a guest spot as the pianist on her song "Everything Is Everything" from her album *The Miseducation of Lauryn Hill.* That 1998 recording marked his first professional credit as a musician.

Lauryn Hill, during her show at the Back2Black Festival at Leopoldina Station in Rio de Janeiro. John played piano on "Everything is Everything."

During his time in Pennsylvania, Legend worked as the music minister of the Bethel A.M.E. Church and worked for three years at Boston Consulting Group. At night, he played nightclubs in Pennsylvania and New York City. His hard work paid off with opportunities to serve as a **session musician** with Alicia Keys, Twista, and Janet Jackson. A roommate from college introduced him to his cousin, a beat master from out of town named Kanye West. The two closely collaborated on numerous songs for one another's projects, as well as for other artists, forging a lasting partnership that has resulted in West producing tracks for every studio album that Legend has recorded.

John Legend served as a session musician for Alicia Keys.

Education Matters, and John Legend Agrees

"I come from a city where 40 percent to 50 percent of our kids drop out of high school. I did well in high school and then went to an Ivy League school, but I was the exception. We need to do more to make sure every kid has a quality education." —John Legend

Legend serves as a member of the board of directors of Teach for America, an effort he joined in 2007. Teach for America aims to provide "equitable and excellent education for all children." It targets low-income or poverty-stricken areas to confront educational inequity by providing qualified teachers from its **corps** to teach for at least two years.

John Legend is heavily involved with Teach for America, an organization that helps to ensure that all children receive a good education.

This corps of teachers works to stem the flood of high school dropouts—1.3 million students in the United States. The majority of those dropouts come from low-income homes, and more than half are students of color. Students from low-income homes are five times more likely than those from middle-income families to fail to graduate, and are six times more likely to fail to graduate than those from higher-income families, according to the National Center for Education Statistics (NCES).

Inspired by the teachings of Martin Luther King, Jr. and his contemporaries and looking for a way to do more to help children in the United States

John Legend is inspired by the teachings of Martin Luther King, Jr.

and abroad, Legend founded the Show Me Campaign in 2007. The nonprofit focuses on educational initiatives and efforts to reduce mass incarceration. The latter include initiatives to reduce or eliminate the school-to-prison pipeline. At this time, the United States incarcerates more individuals than any other country. In fact, the United States has more jails and prisons than colleges and universities.

Scan here to watch a CNN interview with John Legend on education reform and poverty.

Legend draws from the upbringing his parents and maternal grandmother provided. Their family-centered upbringing included community service, church involvement, exposure to art and music, and extra effort on their part to engage their child in learning at home. His family taught through love. That prompted him to ask questions about what made his upbringing in a working-class family with little money to spare different from that of other children in similar circumstances. Legend shared his vision in a graduation speech at the University of Pennsylvania in 2014:

"What would our schools look like if we were committed to love in public? If we cared about every kid in our school system, we would make sure they didn't go to school hungry. We would make sure they had proper health care and counseling. We would make sure they had excellent teachers in every classroom. We would make sure we weren't unfairly suspending them and criminalizing them for minor behavioral problems. We'd make sure all of them had the resources they need."

Growing Up in a Musical Family

In that same speech, Legend provided key insights into how he developed so early and quickly as a musician. His parents providing both a piano and drum kit in the home were key. His maternal grandmother was their church's organist. She began teaching Legend to play piano at age seven. This early immersion in learning music fostered a deep connection with both family and music. The extended family even performed as a group—the Stephens 5. It was the death of his grandmother when he was ten years old that spurred his eventual move to the East Coast for college. Her loss led to his mother entering a depressive state. Their home was not the same after his grandmother's death, and as soon as he could move away from the painful memories, he did.

Becoming a Solo Artist

The move from Ohio to Pennsylvania at 16 years of age took guts but paid off. College provided an education in literature and important musical experiences. Plus, it is where he met Kanye West's cousin,

Through talent and dedication John's solo career has gone from strength to strength.

Chrissy gave birth to their second child Miles in 2018.

garnering him the introduction that helped shape both of their careers. Their friendship, founded in the early 2000s, remains strong today. The two co-write and co-produce.

Becoming John Legend

While he did begin using a pseudonym, Legend, in place of his given surname Stephens, that alteration essentially sums up the "becoming" of John Legend. The musician has remained true to his roots, despite its potentially trite sound. The friendships and business ties he fostered in college and just afterward remain steadfast today.

Although he attends church less often than he did when he was a music minister, he still evidences his faith in God through his music. The family strength he learned from his parents as a young child, he instills now in his own family—now expanded to his wife and two children.

Text-Dependent Questions:

1. What made the singing group with whom John Legend performed in college different?

2. Which music producer has Legend most often worked with, and what was their most recent project together?

3. Which rare award achievement has Legend earned, and for what projects?

Research Project:

Legend attended an Ivy League university. Research these eight universities. Which types of degrees do they offer? Which areas of study can you pursue at each?

MOBO: The Music of Black Origin, or MOBOs, refers to an annual awards show founded in 1996 by Kanya King and Andy Ruffell that honors music made by people of color. The awards are conferred annually in the United Kingdom.

Nonprofit: An organization that provides a service without charging for it.

Revival: A theater term used to refer to a new production of an old play or a similar work.

John Legend at the 2005 BET (Black Entertainment Television) Awards.

Chapter 3

John Legend's Hip-Hop Career, Interests, and Passions in Moments

More Than Just a Musician

John Legend maintains careers in acting, music, and business. He founded his own record label, HomeSchool Records in 2007. He's also founded a multi-issue **nonprofit** to tackle education issues that are important to him. He's worked as a voice and presentation coach on some of television's biggest performer competitions, including *Duets, The X-Factor,* and *The Voice.* He's also such a proud husband and father that his Twitter biography says simply, "Chrissy's husband. Father of Luna & Miles. No relation to Arthur."

The Life of an Actor

John Legend does not limit himself to one career. He's enjoyed acting since his teen years, participating in musical theater and theater productions. He broke into film in 2005 with a small part in the film *Loverboy,*

More than a musician, John Legend is also an actor, campaigner, and businessman.

playing the Memphis Parking Lot Donor. He is credited under his given name of John Stephens.

Although his IMDB profile consists largely of composer and "self" appearances, Legend has begun carving out a place for himself as an actor. So far, the majority of his acting credits consist of video shorts, but he has landed a few roles on television and in films. In 2005, he played Stevie Wonder in the "California Dreamin'" episode of *American Dreams*. He played himself in 2007 in "The Bar Mitzvah" episode of *Curb Your Enthusiasm*.

In 2008, he transitioned back to the silver screen, playing Marcus Hooks in the film *Soul Men*. In 2012, it was back to television for the "New York" episode of *Black Cab Sessions USA*. Legend does not seem to feel a need to decide between television and film and switches back and forth as projects require.

In 2016, he worked on two films, appearing in *La la Land* as Keith and in the television movie *The Toycracker: A Mini-Musical Spectacular* as Rat King. The following year, he guest-starred on two television series. He played Frederick Douglass in the "Whiteface" episode of *Underground* and himself in "The Dinner Party" episode of *Master of None*.

His most recent acting work has netted him major artistic recognition. His 2018 role as Jesus Christ in the television movie *Jesus Christ Superstar Live in Concert* earned him two nominations for

Emmys, one for Outstanding Lead Actor in a Limited Series or Movie and one for Outstanding Variety Special (Live) as a producer of the show. Legend won his first Emmy as a producer for Outstanding Variety Special (Live). He followed up that role by voicing a character for the first time. He voices the character of Crow in the short film *Crow: The Legend*.

Helping Others Get Their Start

From the outset of his career, Legend has worked with others and has collaborated to foster success for all involved. He used the eight years he worked as a session musician before getting signed to learn the business and to study how an artist develops. Three years after getting signed to a recording contract, he started his own label. The first artists he signed to it were Estelle and his brother, Vaughn Anthony. He devoted two years to helping his brother also develop his songwriting skills.

He's worked as a coach on *Duets* in 2012, *The X Factor* in 2014 and 2016, and 2019 season of *The*

John Legend has worked hard to help others fulfill their career dreams.

Voice. Legend continues to find new ways to reach out to young performers to help others get their start in music. He's mentored other artists since the beginning of his career.

Endorsements

BAILEYS IRISH CREAM

In 2008, John Legend began representing Baileys as the brand's celebrity endorser. He lent his face and voice to promote the product. He said he "loved the idea of fans enjoying a glass while listening to his music."

Scan here to watch an interview with Oprah in which John Legend tells when he knew he wanted to marry Chrissy Teigen.

LEXUS

In 2007, Legend filmed a commercial for Lexus, in which he rocks out to a rare performance of Nina Simone singing "Backlash Blues."

GAP

Also in 2007, Legend signed an endorsement agreement with Gap. He represents its product line RED, a for-benefit brand that donates proceeds from sales to help eliminate AIDS in Africa.

Fast Fact 2:

Eliminating AIDS—Improved education is key to preventing AIDS transmission. Currently, in Africa, 64 percent of children are enrolled in primary schools. The percentage lowers in AIDS-affected regions. According to UNAIDS, many African girls do not receive a proper education, which includes information about the epidemic. Scientific studies have revealed that educated females are less likely to contract AIDS and that girls with higher education levels marry later than others. They know more about sexually transmitted diseases, including HIV, and are more likely to seek medical attention and necessary services. African students receive education on HIV infection, transmission, prevention, and treatment. This awareness leads to more conscious safety and prevention behaviors.

HINT WATER

John Legend drank Hint water after picking some up at Whole Foods. He was so impressed with its taste and the real fruit used to flavor the water that he contacted the company. He became an investor during one of its several fundraising rounds. Later on, he also became a brand ambassador. Legend is depicted drinking the water in still photos and videos.

PAMPERS

In 2018, the artist and model Chrissy Teigen joined Pampers as brand endorsers. Both filmed separate commercials for the brand, co-starring their daughter Luna. In Legend's commercial, he sings his "Stinky Booty" song to his daughter. The ad first aired on Father's Day.

Awards Won

John Legend has earned a bevy of accolades for vocal performance, production, and songwriting. He's been honored for his album work, collaborations, and contributions to film soundtracks.

Academy Awards

Best Original Song, "Glory" (with Common) | Won in 2015

African American Film Critics Association

Best Music, "Glory," (with Common) | Won in 2014

American Music Awards (AMAs)

Best New Artist | Won in 2005
Best Collaboration, "Glory," (with Common) | Won in 2015

BET Awards

Best New Artist | Won in 2005
Best Collaboration, "Glory," (with Common) | Won in 2015
Top Rap Album, *Pink Friday: Roman Reloaded* | Won in 2013

Billboard Awards

Top Radio Song, "All of Me" | Won in 2015
Top Streaming Song (Audio), "All of Me" | Won in 2015

Critics' Choice Movie Awards

Best Song, "Glory," (with Common) | Won in 2015

Emmy Awards

Outstanding Variety Special (Live), Jesus Christ Superstar Live in Concert | Won in 2018

Georgia Film Critics Association

Best Original Song, "Glory" (with Common) | Won in 2015

Grammy Awards

Best New Artist, | Won in 2006

Best R&B Album, *Get Lifted* | Won in 2006

Best Male R&B Vocal Performance, "Ordinary People" | Won in 2006

Best Male R&B Vocal Performance, "Heaven" | Won in 2007

Best R&B Performance by a Duo or Group with Vocals, "Family Affair" (with Joss Stone & Van Hunt) | Won in 2007

Best R&B Performance by a Duo or Group with Vocals, "Stay with Me (By the Sea)" (with Al Green) | Won in 2007

Best R&B Song, "Shine" | Won in 2011

Best Traditional R&B Vocal Performance, "Hang On In There" (with The Roots | Won in 2011

Best R&B Album, *Wake Up!* (with The Roots) | Won in 2011

Best Song Written for Visual Media, "Glory" (with Common) | Won in 2016

Mnet Asian Music Awards

International Favorite Artist | Won in 2014

Music of Black Origin (MOBO) Awards

Best R&B Act | Won in 2005

MTV Awards

Best Video with a Social Message, "One Man Can Change the World"
(with Kanye West and Big Sean) | Won in 2015
Best Fight Against the System, "Surefire" | Won in 2017

NAACP Image Awards

Outstanding Song, "All of Me" | Won in 2014
Outstanding Male Artist | Won in 2016

Soul Train Music Awards

Best R&B/Soul Album, Male, *Get Lifted* | Won in 2006
Best R&B/Soul Single, Male, "Ordinary People" | Won in 2006
Best R&B/Soul Single, Male, "Save Room" | Won in 2007
Record of the Year (The Ashford & Simpson Songwriter's Award), "All of Me" |
Won in 2014
Ashford & Simpson Songwriter's Award, "Glory" (with Common) | Won in 2015

Tony Awards

Best **Revival** of a Play, "Jitney" | Won in 2017

John Legend at the NAACP Image Awards in Pasadena, CA. He won awards in both 2014 and 2016.

Success Doesn't Happen Overnight

Determined, genius, and tireless describe the traits leading to Legend's *success*. His dedication to his craft—whether acting, voice, piano, or songwriting—shows in the diversity of his career, projects,

Through hard work, talent, and motivation, John has reached the top of his game.

and collaborations. He began in church choir at age four and earned his first professional credit at 20 years old. It took eight long years of nightclub dates after that, while working a day job and fitting in work as a session musician to land a recording contract. He self-funded and self-released multiple CDs before his first studio album in 2004. Legend had to believe in himself and in what he was doing. He speaks of feeling led to pursue music, even while he was employed by a consulting firm and earning a strong salary. Knowing in his heart that music was his intended path, he dedicated himself to making it his main career.

John Legend HIP-HOP & R&B

Text-Dependent Questions:

1 Discuss with a classmate the various types of acting jobs that Legend has landed. What are the differences among musical theater, theater, film, television, and voiceover work?

2 How has John Legend combined his endorsements and investments?

3 Legend often repeatedly works with certain key musicians. Has he also worked with any actors, actresses, or directors multiple times?

Research Project:

John Legend has built an impressive résumé of music and film credits. Choose one project he produced. Research what goes into producing an album, television show, or single, based upon what you learn about how the Legend project you choose developed.

Words to Understand

Books: In recording, this refers to scheduling. When an artist "books studio time," they reserve and rent a recording studio.

Target markets: The precise group of people a marketer wants to reach with an advertisement or product as defined by factors such as age group, ethnicity, gender, and income.

Webinar: An online seminar or class that streams through a website. Some you must attend as a live event, and others you can stream at any time.

John Legend performing in Rio de Janeiro in 2015.

John Legend

Chapter 4

John Legend's Brand Messaging—
Becoming a Worldwide Sensation

John Legend's Marketing Strategy

As the recording industry changed, so did the marketing methods used by musicians. While marketing once fell to the record company and publicity executives, today's artists must self-promote more than in the past. Until the advent of the Internet, musicians marketed or shopped their demos to record companies. Once signed, the label's publicity department took care of all marketing. The Internet equalized access to fans, providing musicians a direct route to fans, particularly through their own social media accounts and websites.

John Legend recorded two self-published CDs.

The move to the Internet and direct marketing to fans required musicians to learn new skills. Each independent musician became his or her own publicist. During his eight year stint as a session musician, John Legend released two self-published CDs that he marketed on his own.

Once signed to a label, he automatically assisted his label by promoting his music through endorsement opportunities and working partnerships. Legend became a legend at marketing, so much so that he is now booked regularly as a public speaker on the topic. One such instance occurred at Interact 2014, where he delivered the keynote address on marketing. He unromanticized life as a creative person with his advice.

Creativity Is a Job

Hold yourself accountable. Forget about inspiration, and focus on perspiration. Set a schedule, and create or write every day. When Legend has a song due for a project, or an album due to the record company, he **books** studio time and works until he finishes it. Songwriting is his job, and he works at it daily. You must develop discipline to remain consistently creative.

Scan here to watch Common and John Legend's Oscar acceptance speech.

Collaboration Creates Opportunity

Legend's long-time songwriting and producing partnership with Kanye West has benefitted both artists. Both were just starting out when they first met. Not only does collaboration foster chemistry to create a better product, it doubles your marketing opportunities providing two fan bases, two individuals set on success and, if the artists are both signed, two record companies devoting resources to promotion. Build partnerships to improve and extend the reach of your marketing.

Study the Greats and Learn

In relation to music, this meant Legend studied performers such as Aretha Franklin, Nat King Cole, Marvin Gaye, and Stevie Wonder. You elevate your standards by studying the successful people who came before you. Part of marketing is emulating the successful mannerisms, stage presence, and interview techniques of other performers. With more direct respect to marketing, it means studying the great advertisers and marketers, like David Ogilvy, through reading books, blogs, and case studies and watching **webinars**.

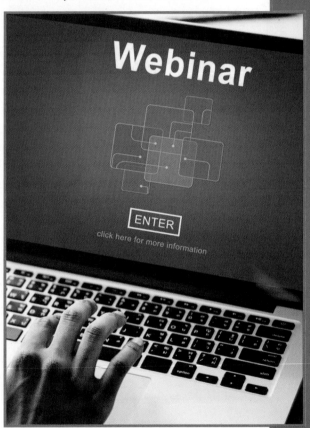

Develop Your Inner Storyteller

In songwriting, Legend develops a story. Successful marketing techniques do the same. Legend is an expert

John learned his craft by studying other performers' blogs and webinars.

balladeer and he writes a break-up song on each record. That's good marketing. People buy what reminds them of themselves, which is why television executives research **target markets** before creating television shows. They created a hit with *Modern Family* by crafting a set of characters who provided the major target audiences with characters who seemed like them. The older father married a younger, attractive Hispanic woman, and they had children. The family includes a gay couple who have adopted their first child. It rounds out with both older and younger family members. The show's creators crafted a guaranteed hit by providing a cast of characters who gave nearly everyone who could potentially watch a character like them with whom to identify. Legend's love songs and break-up songs do the same thing, providing listeners with a shared event to which they can all relate. The story draws them in, and the chorus hooks them.

John Legend always adds a break-up track to his albums because people can relate to them.

Persevere

People do not buy after the first time they see or hear your ad. Legend learned that during the eight years he worked as a session musician, trying to convince record company after record company to sign him. After landing his first professional gig on a Lauryn Hill CD in 1998, he thought he'd be signed within a year. The opposite happened. Every label he approached turned him down—for eight years. He finally got signed in 2004 after having persevered, incessantly shopping his demos and recording numerous featured appearances on other artists' singles. Accept that viewers need to see your ad multiple times before moving completely through the sales funnel.

Study Your Competition

One advantage of Legend's love of collaboration is that it gets him in the same room with the other artists who are also in competition for the Billboard Top 100. While he gets to study the competition up close, most companies require competition analysis and market research for that. Study your competition. Identify their strengths and weaknesses. You can craft a better product than theirs based on that. Market it better than they do. You can even use the same marketing methods with your own spin.

Scan here to watch John Legend discuss collaboration and his many partnerships with Kanye West.

John Legend

Scan here to watch John Legend tell the story of how airport security nearly spoiled his marriage proposal.

Reveal Your Heart

Legend explained that to write a hit love song like "All of Me," he actually had to be in love to write it. Unlike his prior love songs, he wrote "All of Me," about his relationship with his wife. He had to know and understand firsthand what it means to love unconditionally in order to write what became his biggest hit. Its authenticity made it as relatable as its universal topic. Marketing does the same thing. It reaches out to an audience to address a problem its target experiences. It draws in the audience with an authentic, honest message that explains how to solve the problem.

Social Media Tactics

John Legend and his wife, model and author Chrissy Teigen, turn to social media almost daily. He presents a clear message of creativity and family by posting a mix of text, photos and videos to Facebook, Instagram, Twitter and YouTube. These posts convey both his work life and his family life. He and his spouse trade messages on Twitter, tweeting back and forth to one another.

Branding the Name John Legend

Legend has used a combination of in-person appearances, product endorsements and brand ambassadorships, interviews, film

The Issue of Mass Incarceration—Although the United States comprises about 5 percent of the world's population, it houses 21 percent of the world's prisoners. Many of these incarcerations stem from non-violent offenses. Drug-use violations trigger many arrests. Although African Americans and whites participate in drug use at similar rates, the system imprisons African Americans at a rate of nearly six times that of whites. The after-effects of incarceration include reduced employability. Merely having a criminal record reduces the likelihood of an interview callback or job offer by almost 50 percent. For African American applicants, the negative impacts are nearly twice as severe.

and television appearances, and philanthropic works to build his brand beyond and within in the music community. He approaches every aspect of the creative process as a marketing opportunity to build and promote his brand.

In the United States, African Americans are six times more likely to be imprisoned than whites.

John and Chrissy turn to social media on a daily basis—usually posting about work and family life.

Text-Dependent Questions:

❶ Name one marketing method that John Legend uses that you could use in a school fundraising sale or in a campaign for class officer. How would you apply it?

❷ How does Legend scope the competition while building his brand?

❸ Name one aspect of John Legend's social media strategy that you have noticed that many other celebrities do not employ.

Research Project:

Create a mock marketing campaign for a school doughnut or candy bar sale using John Legend's marketing advice. How would you implement his strategies?

Words to Understand

Demo: A three- to five-song CD that an artist uses to market his or her work to record companies and nightclub owners.

Intervention: Taking proactive action to improve a situation.

Poverty cycle: A cycle in which once an individual or community falls into poverty, a set of events or factors will likely continue unless there is outside intervention.

The Show Me Campaign works with children to help break the poverty cycle, so that they don't end up homeless like this man in San Francisco, CA.

Chapter 5

John Legend Reminds Us to Give of Ourselves

Charitable Work: Giving Back to the Community

Legend actively uses his position in music to further social justice issues, a practice he learned from his parents and their community activity. The artist's parents not only volunteered in the community and in the church but also parented foster children. This influence and the development of his own family have made family issues a philanthropic highlight for him.

American Civil Liberties Union

On President Trump's 72nd birthday, Legend and his nuclear family donated $288,000 to the American Civil Liberties Union (ACLU). That amounted to a $72,000 donation each from him, Tiegen, and each of their two children. The symbolic gesture on the part

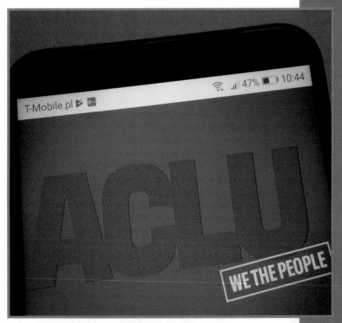

ACLU works to defend and preserve the rights of individuals throughout the United States.

of their infants was meant to drive home the need to protect immigrant families seeking asylum and trying to avoid being separated.

Show Me Campaign

In 2007, Legend founded the Show Me Campaign to help break the **poverty cycle** by providing children access to quality education. It began its initiatives in Africa and the United States. Show Me works to lift people out of poverty via education. It features initiatives geared toward children's education and **interventions** that can redirect prison inmates toward education opportunities.

Helping Individuals Thrive

Although not originally intended as a scholarship program, Legend turned the Show Me Campaign into one. During his initial visit to Ghana, he met a young girl named Rose, who had dropped out of school due to lack of money. Legend described "her energy and her

A good education is the best way to reduce poverty all over the world.

The Show Me Campaign seeks to provide quality education for all children to help them succeed.

Careers in Music–Careers in music extend far beyond that of performing musician. You can teach music, direct a choir, serve as a minister of music, work as a music journalist, score films, manage a venue, or treat people through music therapy, a form of physical and psychiatric therapy.

Funding A Demo Recording—Recording a **demo** of music to shop it to record companies or nightclub owners costs about $1,000 at a minimum. A demo usually consists of three to five songs, about the length of an EP. Each song requires a minimum of two hours of studio time to record, at about $150 per song. The price includes burning the songs to a physical compact disc. The cost of discs and cases and replicating the CDs costs between $400 and $500.

spirit" in later interviews. He chose to fund her secondary school education with a scholarship.

To continue to further these education initiatives, Legend also began serving on the board of directors of Teach for America.

Raising Funds with Partnerships

Legend partnered with The RealReal to offer insights into his style. The website linked his chosen outfits to stores and provided a percentage of sales proceeds to the Show Me Campaign.

How John Legend Reminds Us to Give Back

John Legend volunteers for a number of organizations and serves on the board of directors of one. He involves his entire family in fundraising and philanthropic efforts. He's volunteered at charitable events, such as when he spent a day with Tide washing laundry for hurricane victims. He also dedicates himself to long-term efforts such as founding his own nonprofit.

From an early age, John Legend has been encouraged to give back to the community. He has used his career to further his philanthropic efforts.

John Legend has used his creativity to enhance the lives of others. Today, he continues to inspire and encourage his fans to follow their dreams.

Text-Dependent Questions:

1. What is one philanthropic initiative in which Legend is involved that also interests you?

2. How has his own upbringing influenced Legend's involvement in education philanthropies?

3. Which initiative that John Legend is involved with do your think most benefits the community at large?

Research Project:

Choose one of the major education issues in which Legend is involved, and research how it affects your community. For example, identify the incarceration rates by ethnicity and income level in your community.

Series Glossary of Key Terms

A&R: an abbreviation that stands for Artists and Repertoire, which is a record company department responsible for the recruitment and development of talent; similar to a talent scout for sports.

ambient: a musical style that relies on electronic sounds, gentle music, and the lack of a regular beat to create a relaxed mood for the listener.

brand: a particular product or a characteristic that serves to identify a particular product; a brand name is one having a well-known and usually highly regarded or marketable word or phrase.

cameo: also called a cameo role; a minor part played by a prominent performer in a single scene of a motion picture or a television show.

choreography: the art of planning and arranging the movements, steps, and patterns of dancers.

collaboration: a product created by working with someone else; combining individual talents.

debut: a first public appearance on a stage, on television, or so on, or the beginning of a profession or career; the first appearance of something, like a new product.

deejay (DJ): a slang term for a person who spins vinyl records on a turntable; aka a disc jockey.

demo: a recording of a new song, or of one performed by an unknown singer or group, distributed to disc jockeys, recording companies, and the like, to demonstrate the merits of the song or performer.

dubbed: something that is named or given a new name or title; in movies, when the actors' voices have been replaced with those of different performers speaking another language; in music, transfer or copying of previously recorded audio material from one medium to another.

endorsement: money earned from a product recommendation, typically by a celebrity, athlete, or other public figure.

entrepreneur: a person who organizes and manages any enterprise, especially a business, usually with considerable initiative and at financial risk.

falsetto: a man singing in an unnaturally high voice, accomplished by creating a vibration at the very edge of the vocal chords.

genre: a subgroup or category within a classification, typically associated with works of art, such as music or literature.

hone, honing: sharpening or refining a set of skills necessary to achieve success or perform a specific task.

icon: a symbol that represents something, such as a team, a religious person, a location, or an idea.

innovation: the introduction of something new or different; a brand-new feature or upgrade to an existing idea, method, or item.

instrumental: serving as a crucial means, agent, or tool; of, relating to, or done with an instrument or tool.

jingle: a short verse, tune, or slogan used in advertising to make a product easily remembered.

mogul: someone considered to be very important, powerful, and in charge; a term usually associated with heads of businesses in the television, movie studio, or recording industries.

performing arts: skills that require public performance, as acting, singing, or dancing.

philanthropy: goodwill to fellow members of the human race; an active effort to promote human welfare.

public relations: the activity or job of providing information about a particular person or organization to the public so that people will regard that person or organization in a favorable way.

sampler: a digital or electronic musical instrument, related to a synthesizer, that uses samples, or sound recordings, of real instruments (trumpet, violin, piano, etc.) mixed with excerpts of recorded songs and other interesting sounds (sirens, ocean waves, construction noises, car horns, etc.) that are stored digitally and can be replayed by a triggering device, like a sequencer, electronic drums, or a MIDI keyboard.

single: a music recording having two or more tracks that is shorter than an album, EP, or LP; also, a song that is particularly popular, independent of other songs on the same album or by the same artist.

Further Reading

Legend, John. *Best of John Legend: Updated Edition.* Hal Leonard. 2017

Legend, John. *Best of John Legend—Easy Piano.* Hal Leonard. 2017.

Hinman, Bonnie. *John Legend.* Mitchell Lane Publishers. 2010.

Legend, John. *Evolver Songbook.* Cherry Lane Music Company. 2009.

Legend, John. *Get Lifted Songbook.* Cherry Lane Music Company. 2005.

Internet Resources

www.billboard.com
The official site of Billboard Music, with articles about artists, chart information, and more.

www.thefader.com
Official website for a popular New York City–based music magazine.

www.hiphopweekly.com
A young-adult hip-hop magazine.

www.thesource.com
Website for a bi-monthly magazine that covers hip-hop and pop culture.

https://www.instagram.com/johnlegend
John Legend's official Instagram for all the latest photos.

https://twitter.com/johnLegend
John Legend's official Twitter for all the latest news and updates.

https://www.johnlegend.com
John Legend's official website—the go-to source for all official updates and music.

Citations

"John Legend – Live at SOB's." Discogs. Accessed January 15, 2019.
https://www.discogs.com/John-Legend-Live-At-SOBs/release/3570328

"John Legend—Live at SOB's." All Music. Accessed January 15, 2019. https://www.allmusic.com/album/live-at-sobs-new-york-city-mw0000030854

"Solo Sessions, Vol. 1: Live at the Knitting Factory." All Music. Accessed January 15, 2019. https://www.allmusic.com/album/solo-sessions-vol-1-live-at-the-knitting-factory-mw0001900205

"Live at the Tin Angel: Legend Network CD Volume 1." Discogs. Accessed January 15, 2019.
https://www.discogs.com/John-Legend-Live-At-The-Tin-Angel-Legend-Network-CD-Volume-1/release/11579543

"Evolver." All Music. Accessed January 15, 2019.
https://www.allmusic.com/album/evolver-mw0000799573

"Live from Philadelphia." All Music. Accessed January 15, 2019. https://www.allmusic.com/album/live-from-philadelphia-mw0000582845

"Legend Network: John Legend 2008." Discogs. Accessed January 15, 2019. https://www.discogs.com/John-Legend-Legend-Network-John-Legend-2008/release/11682137

"Wake Up!" All Music. Accessed January 15, 2019.
https://www.allmusic.com/album/wake-up%21-mw0002024479

"Love in the Future." Pop Matters. Accessed January 15, 2019. https://www.popmatters.com/175331-john-legend-love-in-the-future-2495723835.html

"Darkness and Light." All Music. Accessed January 15, 2019.
https://www.allmusic.com/album/darkness-and-light-mw0002995855

"A Legendary Christmas." All Music. Accessed January 15, 2019. https://www.allmusic.com/album/a-legendary-christmas-mw0003214459

"John Legend." encyclopedia.com. Accessed January 16, 2019. https://www.encyclopedia.com/people/literature-and-arts/music-popular-and-jazz-biographies/john-legend

Mitchell, Gail. "John Legend & Blake Mills on Recording 'Darkness and Light': There Will Be No 'Songs About Nothing.'" Billboard. November 17, 2016. https://www.billboard.com/articles/columns/hip-hop/7581265/john-legend-blake-mills-darkness-light-interview

"A Legendary Christmas with John and Chrissy." NBC. Accessed January 16, 2019.
https://www.nbc.com/a-legendary-christmas-with-john-and-chrissy

"John Legend." IMDB. Accessed January 16, 2019.
https://www.imdb.com/name/nm1775466/?ref_=nv_sr_1

"John Legend's Brother, Vaughn Anthony, Ready for Spotlight." Billboard. Accessed January 16, 2019.
https://www.billboard.com/articles/news/268664/john-legends-brother-vaughn-anthony-ready-for-spotlight

"Statistics on How Poverty Affects Children in Schools." Seattle P-I. Accessed January 17, 2019.
https://education.seattlepi.com/statistics-poverty-affects-children-schools-3636.html

"John Legend has signed on to serve as celebrity endorser for liquor Baileys Irish Cream." Ace Showbiz. January 28, 2008.
https://aceshowbiz.com/news/view/00013773.html

Krew. "John Legend & Nina Simone Star in Lexus Mark Levinson Commercial." Lexus Enthusiast. June 15th, 2007.
https://lexusenthusiast.com/2007/06/15/john-legend-nina-simone-star-in-lexus-mark-levinson-commercial/

"Gap Introduces Inspirational Marketing Campaign to Celebrate First Anniversary of Global Launch of Gap (Product) Red." Gap Inc. Oct. 3, 2007.
http://www.gapinc.com/content/gapinc/html/media/pressrelease/2007/med_pr_REDmarketing100307.html

Hochman, David. "Why John Legend and other investors poured millions into a beverage start-up inspired by Coke." CNBC. June 20, 2017.
https://www.cnbc.com/2017/06/20/why-john-legend-and-other-investors-poured-millions-into-a-beverage-start-up-inspired-by-coke.html

"John Legend sings the 'Stinky Booty' song to his daughter in Father's Day ad for Pampers." Marketing Industry News. June 14, 2018.
https://marketingindustrynews.com/2018/06/14/john-legend-sings-the-stinky-booty-song-to-his-daughter-in-fathers-day-ad-for-pampers/

Davis, Phil. "3 Marketing Takeaways from John Legend." Tower Data. August 06, 2014.
https://www.towerdata.com/blog/bid/207408/3-Marketing-Takeaways-from-John-Legend

Newman, Daniel. "John Legend: Insights On Modern Marketing #Interact14." Fow Media. July 18, 2014.
https://fowmedia.com/john-legend-insights-modern-marketing-interact14/

Salway, Chris. "Is John Legend a Marketing Genius?" Progrexion. August 13, 2014.
https://www.progrexion.com/blog/marketing/is-john-legend-a-marketing-genius.html

Batista, Amanda. "6 tips from John Legend to help your strategy 'get lifted.'" Oracle Modern Marketing Blog. July 17, 2014.
https://blogs.oracle.com/marketingcloud/6-tips-john-legend-help-strategy-get-lifted

Kannangara, Rashini Wijesinghe. "What Can Be Done to Stop the Spread of AIDS Among African Children?" The York Review. Accessed January 17, 2019.
https://www.york.cuny.edu/academics/writing-program/the-york-scholar-1/volume-5.2-spring-2009/what-can-be-done-to-stop-the-spread-of-aids-among-african-children

"Criminal Justice Fact Sheet." NAACP. Accessed January 17, 2019.
https://www.naacp.org/criminal-justice-fact-sheet/

Hearon, Sarah. "Chrissy Teigen, John Legend and Their Kids Donate $72,000 Each to ACLU on Donald Trump's Birthday." USA Magazine. June 14, 2018.
https://www.usmagazine.com/celebrity-news/news/chrissy-teigen-john-legend-donate-to-aclu-on-donald-trumps-birthday/

"Music Careers." Careers in Music. Accessed January 17, 2019. https://www.careersinmusic.com/music-careers/

Hume, Jody. "John Legend on His Style & Giving Back With the Show Me Campaign." Real Style. November 18, 2014.
https://realstyle.therealreal.com/john-legend-style-show-me-campaign/

Howell, Sam. "Four Ways John Legend Inspires Us All by Using His Platform for Good." E! Online. November 3, 2018.
https://www.eonline.com/shows/peoples_choice_awards/news/980709/four-ways-john-legend-inspires-us-all-by-using-his-platform-for-good

"Tide—Loads of Hope." Tide. Accessed January 17, 2019.
https://tide.com/en-us/about-tide/loads-of-hope

How Much Does a Good Music Studio Cost to Use? Recording Connection. Accessed January 17, 2019.
https://www.recordingconnection.com/reference-library/recording-entrepreneurs/how-much-do-music-studios-cost/

Educational Video Links

Chapter 1:
http://x-qr.net/1HuM
http://x-qr.net/1JGA
http://x-qr.net/1JM4
http://x-qr.net/1JBY
http://x-qr.net/1Ksp
http://x-qr.net/1K65
http://x-qr.net/1Ldb

Chapter 2:
http://x-qr.net/1JgT
http://x-qr.net/1KMc

Chapter 3:
http://x-qr.net/1LeU
http://x-qr.net/1Jn1

Chapter 4:
http://x-qr.net/1KTq

Index

Index

Index

Picture Credits

Chapter 1:
Twocoms | Shutterstock.com
Atl360Pic | Shutterstock.com
Kathy Hutchins | Shutterstock.com
Everett Collection | Shutterstock.com
S_Bukley | Shutterstock.com
Sean Nel | Shutterstock.com
Jaguar PS | Shutterstock.com
S_Bukley | Shutterstock.com
J Stone | Shutterstock.com
Rena Schild | Shutterstock.com
Alessia Pierdomenico | Shutterstock.com
Featureflash Photo Agency | Shutterstock.com
Featureflash Photo Agency | Shutterstock.com
Kathy Hutchins | Shutterstock.com
Christian Bertrand | Shutterstock.com
Kristopher Kettner | Shutterstock.com
Ron Adar | Shutterstock.com
A. PAES | Shutterstock.com

Chapter 2:
Featureflash Photo Agency | Shutterstock.com
S_Bukley | Shutterstock.com
Tinseltown | Shutterstock.com
A. PAES | Shutterstock.com
Kathy Hutchins | Shutterstock.com
ESB Professional | Shutterstock.com
Wikimedia Commons | Public Domain
Art4alll | Shutterstock.com
Atl360Pic | Shutterstock.com
Kathy Hutchins | Shutterstock.com

Chapter 3:
Featureflash Photo Agency | Shutterstock.com
Sean Nel | Shutterstock.com
Wikimedia Commons | Fair Use
J Stone | Shutterstock.com

Matthew Clemente | Shutterstock.com
Kathy Hutchins | Shutterstock.com
Tinseltown | Shutterstock.com

Chapter 4:
Andre Luiz Moreira | Shutterstock.com
Cabreafoto | Shutterstock.com
Raw Pixel | Shutterstock.com
Sean Nel | Shutterstock.com
Joesph Sohm | Shutterstock.com
Lev Radin | Shutterstock.com
Kathy Hutchins | Shutterstock.com

Chapter 5:
ChamelelonsEye | Shutterstock.com
Pitr Swat | Shutterstock.com
Monkey Business Images | Shutterstock.com
Monkey Business Images | Shutterstock.com
Tinseltown | Shutterstock.com
Lev Radin | Shutterstock.com
Tinseltown | Shutterstock.com
Lev Radin | Shutterstock.com

Front cover:
S_Bukley | Shutterstock.com

Video Credits

http://x-qr.net/1HuM/John Legend
http://x-qr.net/1JGA/blacktreetv
http://x-qr.net/1JM4/John Legend
http://x-qr.net/1JBY/John Legend
http://x-qr.net/1Ksp /John Legend
http://x-qr.net/1K65 /John Legend
http://x-qr.net/1Ldb /John Legend
http://x-qr.net/1JgT/CNN
http://x-qr.net/1KMc/OWN
http://x-qr.net/1LeU /DeeperGraphicWeb
http://x-qr.net/1Jn1/OWN
http://x-qr.net/1KTq/OWN

Author's Biography

Carlie Lawson began writing professionally in 1991. She spent five years at a mid-sized daily newspaper, beating deadline on a daily basis while covering politics and entertainment. She has written for monthly magazines, weekly blogs, and academic publications. Educated at the University of Oklahoma, Carlie holds Bachelor's degrees in Journalism & Mass Communication, and in Film & Video Studies as well as a Master of Regional & City Planning. Carlie owns a consulting firm and conducts research in the area of natural and environmental planning. She also owns a public relations firm. She enjoys hiking, travel, reading, music, guitar, her cat, and the positive-thinking process. Learn more at https://www.writeraccess.com/writer/13038/.